Favorite Zoo Animals Book I

by

Marcia R. Pope

Published by
Marcia R. Pope
Thornton, CO 80229
simpress1@hotmail.com

Table of Contents

Penguins are fun to watch because
they waddle when they walk.
They live together in large groups.
They do not fly but they are very good
swimmers. They hear very well too,
even though you can't see their ears.

Dall Sheep live way high up
in the mountains and are good climbers.
Both the male and the female sheep have
big curly horns. You can tell how old they
are by the number of rings on their horns.
They have white wooly coats to keep them
warm when it's cold.

The **Cheetah** is part of the cat family.
They can purr but they cannot roar.
They have excellent eyesight during the
day and can see for long distances.
Did you know that cheetahs can run faster
than any other animal in the world? They
can run up to 75 miles an hour!

Here is an animal called the **Lesser Kudu**.
The Kudu is a type of antelope.
They are from Africa and they like to hide
in the woodlands. They have white stripes
and spots on their body and the male kudus
have long spiral horns. Kudus can leap up to
6 feet if they need to. They like to eat
grass, fruit, and plants.

This big animal is a **Brown Bear**.
They are also called grizzly bears and
some can weigh up to 1400 pounds.
When they stand up on their hind legs
they can be up to 7 feet tall.
Brown bears like to fish. They have long
sharp claws too, so watch out!

There are many birds at the zoo.
This one is a tropical bird known as a
Nicobar Pigeon. They are from southeast
Asia and like to live in hot humid places
and wooded forests. They eat fruit, seeds
and small insects. Look at his colorful
green, blue and gold feathers!

These two **Mississippi Map Turtles** are walking slowly. They spend a lot of their time sitting on rocks taking a sun bath or going for a swim. Turtles are excellent swimmers. Many turtles hide inside of their shell if they sense danger.

The **Giraffe** has a very long neck and long thin legs. They are the tallest animals in the zoo. Giraffes have very long tongues and they can reach high up in the trees. They like to eat leaves and plants. Did you know that every giraffe has a different spot pattern?

Peacocks like to walk around the zoo.
The male peacock has beautiful feathers in
his tail with colors of blue, green, gold and
red. Their tail is called a train. It can be up
to five feet long. The male spreads their
tail feathers very wide like this when they
want to attract the female peacocks.
Did you know that a peacock can fly?

This animal is called a **Somali Wild Ass**.
He belongs to the donkey family.
He has excellent hearing.
He likes to eat grass, tree bark
and leaves. When he says, "Hee-haw!", his
voice is very loud! He can be heard
almost 2 miles away.

There are many different types of
birds at the zoo. These two birds are
African Pygmy Falcons.
They all have pretty colors.
They are about eight inches long.
They have a funny habit of bobbing
their heads up and down just before
they catch their prey.

There are different types of **Monkeys** at the zoo. Monkeys are fun to watch. They like to play in the trees. Monkeys can swing from branch to branch with no problem. Sometimes they come down to the ground to get some food. A big group of monkeys is called a troop.

The **Elephant** is a very big animal. When he is thirsty he can pull water into his trunk and squirt it into his mouth. Elephants use their trunk for smelling, breathing, grabbing things, and for making a loud noise called trumpeting. Elephants are also very good swimmers.

There are many different kinds of fish
at the zoo. Some are very tiny and
some are pretty big. This big green
fish is called a **Peacock Bass**.
Look at his rich green color!
Peacock bass live in warm
tropical water.

The **Dik-Dik** is a miniature antelope. They come from different parts of Africa. They stand less than two feet tall and some people keep them as pets. Dik-Diks usually live in pairs. When they are in danger they run in a zig-zig pattern and send out a whistling sound. They like to eat grass, fruit and berries.

This a **Mexican Spiny-tailed Iguana**. He is a type of lizard. He likes to eat insects, fruits and vegetation. Iguanas use their tail to help defend themselves. The color of this iguana helps him to blend in well with his surroundings. Can you see him?

This bird is a called a
Snowy Crowned Robin Chat.
He normally lives in tropical areas and
the African woodlands.
Many birds in the zoo like this one are
kept in glass enclosures.

Snow Leopards belong to the cat family.
Their tail is almost as long as their body
and they can use it to keep their balance.
They usually live in high mountainous
areas and they don't mind the snow.
Their fur is about 5 inches thick.
Snow leopards are rather shy animals.

The feathers of the **Flamingo** bird are beautiful bright shades of pink. Flamingos have very skinny legs and their knees bend backwards. They like to flock in large groups called colonies and they can be pretty noisy. When they want to rest they stand on one leg.

The **Bighorn Sheep** have curly horns but only the male sheep have these horns. This bighorn sheep is taking a rest right now, but if he needs to, he can climb very steep rocks with no problem. They live together in large groups known as a herd. Bighorn sheep have excellent eyesight.

This big animal is a **Hippopotamus**.
He is from Africa. He is called a Hippo
for short. He spends a lot of time in the
water. He can weigh up to 4,000 pounds!
Believe it or not, he really doesn't eat as
much as you think. Did you know that
hippos can run faster than you can?

This animal is called a **Bongo**.
Bongos are from Africa and they are part
of the antelope family. They like to group
together in large numbers. They have red
chestnut colored coats with white
stripes. They eat leaves, bushes, roots,
shrubs, rotten trees, and fruit.

Black Bears are very agile.
They are excellent climbers and they can climb trees with no problem. They are also good swimmers. They have very big paws and their claws give them a good grip for climbing. They like to eat grass, berries, fish, and insects.

Polar Bears live in cold climates like the Artic. They actually have black skin but their fur looks white. They eat mostly seals and can smell food a mile away. This bear is having fun bouncing up and down on a blue barrel.

This animal is called a **Sea Lion**. Their skin is black and slippery. They walk using their flippers but they are excellent swimmers. They have good vision both above water and under water. They eat different types of fish.

The End

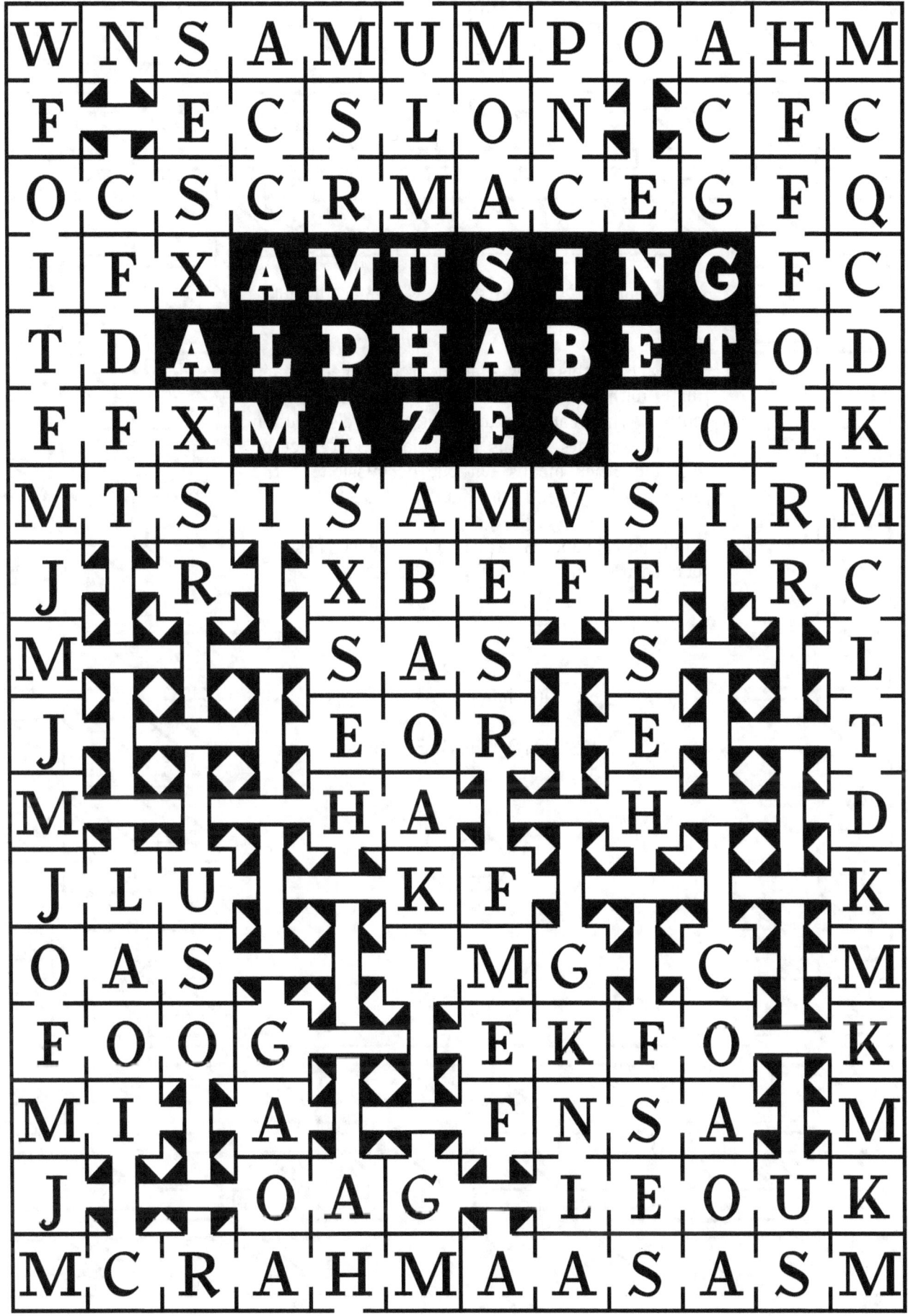

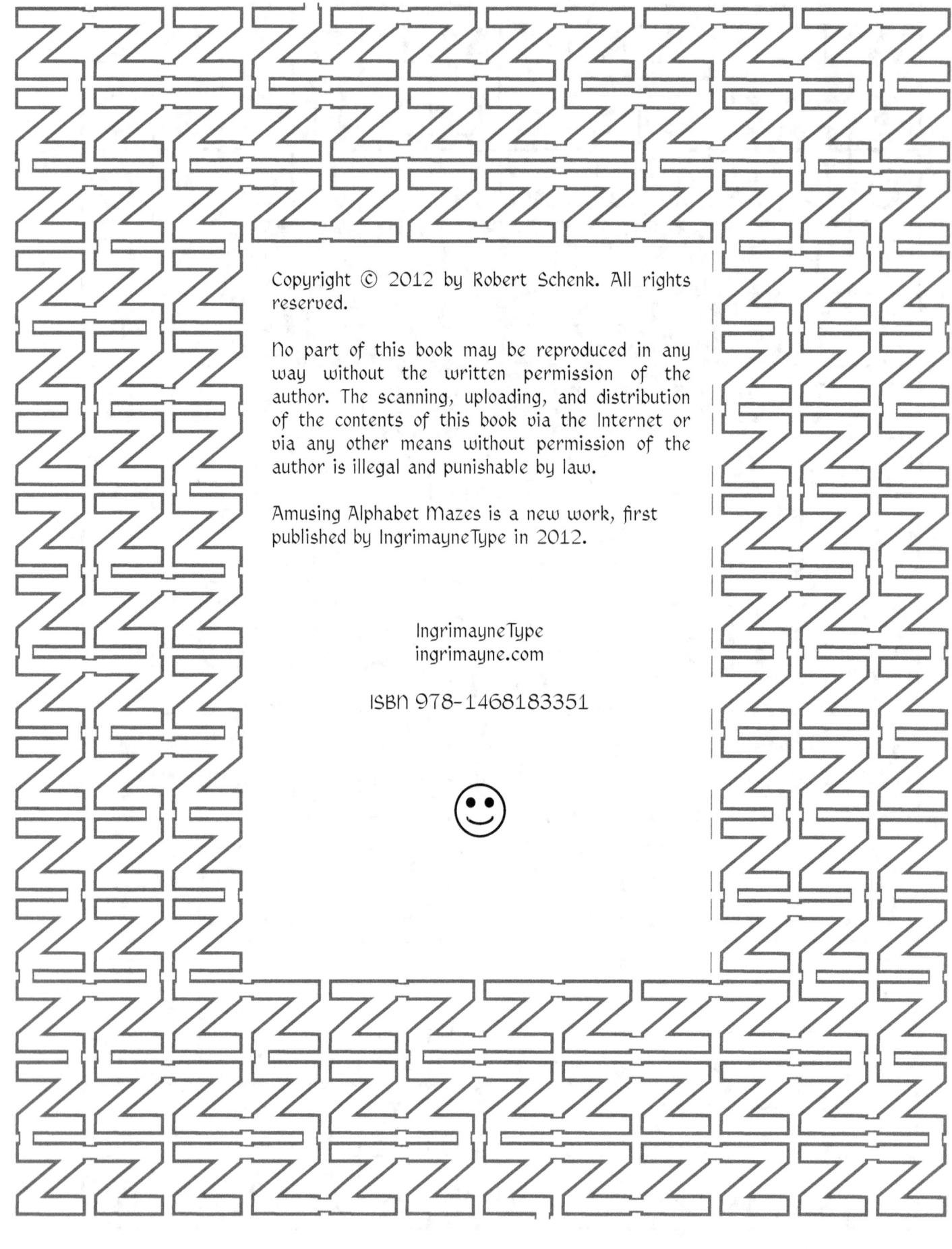

Amusing Alphabet Mazes is a new work, first published by IngrimayneType in 2012.

IngrimayneType
ingrimayne.com

ISBN 978-1468183351